TRIVIA FOR KIDS
WHO LOVE CATS

170+ Facts to Engage Smart, Curious Cat Lovers
& Trade "I'm Bored" for Fun and Learning

An Animal Educational Gift and Activity

ASH MALARKEY

TABLE OF CONTENTS

Introduction

What has four legs, two eyes, one nose, and purrs?

It's a cat! Big cats, small cats, house cats, wild cats have been fascinating humans for a very long time.

Have you ever dressed up as a cat for Halloween? Have you dressed your cat up for Halloween? Do you watch cute cat videos online? Have you ever wondered why your cat does the funny things that it does?

Who is more curious—you, or your cat?

Cats can seem like mysterious creatures, but they have a lot of patterns in common that make them easy to understand. We just have to listen to what they are trying to tell us.

Inside this book, you will discover whether black cats are lucky or unlucky, what country worshiped cat gods, what food cats can't get enough of, and which cat was mayor of an entire town.

You will learn about what big cats and small cats have in common, how cat bodies are different or similar to human bodies, and what foods never to feed a cat.

Why do cats hiss? What tail shape means your cat is happy? Which cats won the Guinness Book of World Records, and for which record?

Keep reading and you will find out!

Now, there are so many fun facts about cats that I couldn't include them all in one book, so this is Volume 1. Volume 2 has even more facts, even more cats, and more advanced knowledge.

This book, Volume 1, is an introduction to the magical and mischievous world of cats.

Whether you know a little about cats or a lot, you are bound to learn something new that you can share with the people you love in your life and show them how smart you are!

Hi, friend! I'm Ash. I'm a writer and a big fan of knowledge and animals. For me, there's nothing cooler than learning and spending time with animals. I wrote this book because I love trivia, fun facts, and cats. I learned so much in writing this book, and I can't wait to share these amazing facts with you.

When you are in a long car ride and asking "are we there yet?", or at home and waiting for dinner, or saying "I'm bored!", you can read this book to be entertained and learn something at the same time.

This is trivia, so this book is active and interactive. You will be shouting out answers throughout the whole book–playing games including "True or False," "This or that," and single question and answer. At the end of the book are two extra challenges called the lightning rounds.

There are two lightning quiz rounds at the end—easy and hard. These speedy questions and answers will have no explanations and will jump between topics, out of order, to test your sense of recall and see what fun facts you remember. See how fast you can go through them!

And if you love the facts but forget them, you can come back and read this book as many times as you want!

Trivia is fun for the whole family. You can take turns asking the questions and saying the answers. Or you can all play together and ask the questions out loud and see if any of you can shout out the answer.

You can read this all at once on a long road trip, or you can read a chapter every night before bed to dream about cats and all this new knowledge you have.

Some of the facts have some bigger words and science behind it. If you don't understand everything when you read it, that is okay! You can ask a grown up what something means, or even look it up if you know how to do that. Even if you don't understand every word, you will still be learning a lot!

The more you know about something, the more you appreciate it. So if you have a cat, or want a cat, or just love looking at cats from far away, what you learn here will help you love cats even more—and, may make your cat feel closer to you, too.

If you are a curious kid—of any age—and you want to learn some things, you are in the right place.

Paws up, claws down, meows ready. Let's play cat trivia!

COLORING BOOK

As a free bonus, here is a link to get a printable coloring ebook where you can color in your own cats! Enjoy your coloring!

You can scan the QR code with your phone camera or QR reader.

1
CAT MYTHS: BUSTED

What are some myths you have heard about cats?

First, what is a myth?

According to Merriam-Webster dictionary, which is a helpful book and website to look at to find what different words mean, a myth is "an unfounded or false notion." Basically, a myth is an idea that is not true.

Even though the myth is not true, it is usually something that we have heard many times. But remember, not everything we hear is true. It is always best to check a dictionary, encyclopedia, or other strong research to make sure that we know what is true, and what is false.

So, what have we heard about cats? Let's play a game called "true or false." I'm going to ask a question, and when you know it, I want you to yell out TRUE or FALSE, and then read what the right answer is.

Let's bust some myths and find out what the real facts are about cats.

Are you ready? Here we go!

Question 1: Dogs are more popular pets than cats

A dog is a man's best friend. But what about cats? Can cats be best friends, too?

True or false? Dogs are more popular pets than cats.

Did you get it?

The answer is… FALSE.

The American Pet Products Association estimates that there are 78 million pet dogs in the United States and 86 million pet cats in the United States. There are millions more pet cats than pet dogs in the United States! A million is a very large number—so big that most humans can't even imagine how big one million is. And there are many more millions of cats than dogs that are pets!

Here's where it gets a little tricky. The same organization says that 44% of all households in the United States have a pet dog, but only 35% of households in the United States have a pet cat. So, even though there are more pet cats, fewer houses have cats than dogs. How?

What could this mean?

If there are more pet cats, but a higher percentage of households have dogs, this sounds like a challenging math problem! Many houses have just one pet dog, and that's it. But many households have more than one cat—or even, one dog and several cats. Some people have ten cats or more, all just in one home! Can you imagine a house full of many cats? Do you know anyone with more than one cat? Do you have more than one pet cat in your house?

More families are likely to have a dog than a cat, but if they do have a cat, they may have several cats—which certainly more than makes up for the households who sadly do not have a pet cat!

Cats are the winner here as the most popular pet.

Question 2: Cats love milk

You've seen the cartoons, right? Of cats lapping up milk from the bowl, enjoying themselves. But is it true? Cats love milk.

The answer is… FALSE!

Cats are lactose intolerant—just like many of us humans. This means that after they grow up and don't need the milk from their mommies anymore, their little bodies lose the ability to process the compounds in milk. Even if cats like the taste of milk, if they drink milk or have yogurt or cheese, they could have bad tummy problems.

It's best to stick to food made especially for cats, in order to make your kitty as happy and comfortable as possible, and save milk as a very rare treat, in small amounts, or avoid it altogether, so that your cat has a happy stomach.

So when your cat is thirsty, water is the best idea, since cats need water as much as humans do! Like humans, cats' bodies are made up of 60-70% water. Water is the purr-fect drink for your cat. And when your cat wants a treat, cat treats are the way to go. Let's save the pictures of cats lapping up milk for cartoons so that the cats in our lives can stay happy and healthy.

Question 3: Black cats are bad luck

Like Friday the 13th, stepping on certain cracks in the sidewalk, and broken mirrors, black cats are often seen as bad luck. After all, in any Halloween cartoon, in addition to the orange pumpkins carved with eyes and crooked smiles, and ghosts and witches flying in the air, you will see a black cat with its fur standing straight up and its back arched.

Scary stuff, huh?

So, black cats are bad luck. True or false.

The answer is… FALSE!

First of all, black cats are beautiful. Have you seen a black cat? Or maybe you have a black cat. They can be silly, sweet, moody, everything a cat can be.

In the United States, they have been seen as bad luck. This came from the long history of Halloween, which is a modern interpretation of a very old Gaelic festival in ancient Ireland, called Samhain. In the Celtic festival, there was a story about a very large black cat, and this cat had a white spot on its otherwise black chest. The cat acted as a judge! If a family left out a saucer of milk for the cat to drink, the cat would bless the house. If the family forgot to leave out the milk, the cat would curse the house! Spooky! This is how the idea of black cats being bad luck came to the United States.

But even though the United States has a lot of cats, there are 600 million cats in the whole wide world! That is a lot of cats. And much of the world loves cats!

In Germany, depending on what direction the cat walks in front of you, you will have good luck or bad luck.

In ancient Egypt, black cats were thought to bring good luck! They were worshiped and given the respect that cats know they deserve!

Black cats are also seen as lucky in the United Kingdom including England, way down under in Australia, and throughout various parts of Asia including Japan. In Scotland, a cat at your door may mean that you will receive money.

So if you have a black cat, or you see a black cat, you can feel comfortable knowing that many people think that you are a very lucky person, just for being around the cat! Certainly, the cat thinks that you are lucky to be in the cat's presence! And you are lucky to have the love of the cat.

Question 4: A group of cats is called a cattle

What do you call a group of cats? Is it cattle?

True or false? A group of cats is called a cattle.

The answer is… FALSE.

Cattle refers to a group of cows or bulls, and may even include other animals that eat grass, such as bison, yaks, and buffalos.

So what is a group of cats?

Now, these may sound silly, but these names are TRUE!

A group of cats is called a clowder! No, not chowder. Clowder!

But that's not all. There are many more names for a group of cats. A group of cats is a clowder, yes. It is also a clutter and a glaring. For wild, feral cats, these groups of cats can be called a dowt and a destruction.

Destruction! It seems like the person who named this group of cats had some experience with many mischievous cats!

Do you want to know more cat vocabulary? It doesn't end here!

A group of kittens is called …. Can you guess? A kindle.

No, not the ebook reader from Amazon. A kindle is a group of kittens!

So we have the clowder for the group of adult cats, and many other names. And a kindle for a group of kittens.

For even more cat vocabulary, individual cats have their own names, too. A male cat can be called a tom. But, if the male is neutered and ready to be in your home, the male cat can be called a gib. And a female cat can be called a molly, just like the girl's name molly. And what do you have if you have a tom, a molly, and a gib, and they are all adult cats? A clowder.

See, cats are smart. Very intelligent creatures. And when you learn about cats, you get smarter too. But if you can't remember all the names for the different types of cats, you know what you can say? Cat. Cat is a great name for a cat, and works every time.

Question 5: People who are allergic to cats are allergic to their fur

If you have a cat allergy or know someone who does, you know how tough it is to be sneezing, have red, itchy eyes, irritated skin, and feel so uncomfortable when you just want to spend time with cats!

But some people think that they are allergic to cat fur.

Is that TRUE or FALSE? People who are allergic to cats are allergic to their fur.

Tell me. What is it?

The answer is… FALSE.

People who have cat allergies aren't actually allergic to the cat's fur. What they are allergic to is a protein that is inside almost every one of the cat's functions.

The protein is called Fel d 1, and it is inside of a cat's saliva, its spit. It's inside the urine, the pee. And it's inside the dander, which is something that the cat sheds, kind of like dandruff.

The protein is so small that it is one-tenth the size of a dust allergen. Wow! That's really small. Because it's so small, it's easier for cat allergens to stay in the air, which means that we breathe it in.

But, fun fact: all cats do not have the same amount of the protein! The cats that have the most Fel d 1 are non-neutered males. The cats that make the least amount of this protein are certain breeds including Balinese and Siberian cats. And these breeds are not fur-less cats!

Cat Myths Busted Mini-Quiz

Here is your recap question for busting cat myths:

What is a clowder, a clutter, and a glaring?

Do you remember?

It's a group of cats!

Now that we have busted some myths of what is true and what is false for cats, let's look at where cats come from. What do lions, tigers, and your pet cat have in common? Keep reading to find out!

2
CATS IN THE WILD

Your cat can be silly, cranky, angry, sleepy, but did you know that your cat has a lot of things in common with lions?

Let's learn about these little lions!

For this game, I will ask one question and read two answers, and you will choose the correct answer!

Question 1: What is a big cat?

Is it...

A: Lions, tigers, jaguars, leopards, snow leopards, and even cheetahs and cougars

B: Elephants, rhinos, hippopotami, giraffes, zebras, and even goats and elks

Do you have it? Ready for the answer?

The answer is... A!

Lions, tigers, jaguars, leopards, snow leopards, and even cheetahs and cougars are called big cats. The cat in your home is a small cat. But they are all part of the same cat family! Wild, right?

Let's learn more!

Question 2: How much of a house cat's genetic makeup is the same as that of tigers?

That means, how similar is a cat's body, what it looks like and what it's like inside of its body, is it to the body of a tiger?

Is it…

A: 50%. Your little cat is basically half-tiger!

B: 95.6%. Your cat is almost all tiger!

Do you have it? Ready for the answer?

The answer is… B!

Your cat and tigers share almost all of the same genes! This can explain why your cat might have some of the same behaviors as big cats, even though your cat lives an easy life of sleeping and being fed! Your cat may pounce, stalk prey like mice, and mark its territory—just like tigers do!

Question 3: What is the name of the cat family?

Is it…

A: Canidae

B: Felidae

Do you have it? Ready for the answer?

The answer is… B!

Big cats—and cats like the ones that live in many homes!—are all part of the same biological family called *Felidae*. Felidae is the name of the family, and there is another word you may have heard—feline—that describes all of these cats.

Now let's get into some of the genus groups of cats. What is a genus? No, not a genius! A genus is a category that groups together similar things: in this case, types of cats. The plural of genus, fun fact, is *genera*! If you want to study biology and learn more about people, animals, and plants, you will learn about all types of genera!

So how are cats divided into categories? Let's take a look!

Question 4: The Panthera genus includes lions, tigers, leopards, snow leopards, jaguars, and—you guessed it—panthers! What is an unmistakable sign of the Panthera genus?

Is it...

A: They roar!

B: They sleep a lot!

Do you have it? Ready for the answer?

The answer is... A! They roar.

This was a bit of a trick question because the cats do sleep a lot! Just like house cats, big cats spend a lot of their time sleeping! But since all cats sleep a lot, that is not a sign that they are part of the Panthera genus.

What makes the Panthera cats different is that they roar! Think about *The Lion King* or other stories of these big cats showing their teeth and roaring! Or maybe you've seen videos on YouTube. Your cat may meow, hiss, and growl, but your cat does not roar like the Panthera genus.

But there are two more groups of cats! What are they?

Question 5: What big cat is the only living cat in the genus Acinonyx?

Is it...

A: The cheetah

B: The jungle cat

Do you have it? Ready for the answer?

The answer is... A! The cheetah.

Way back 10,000 years ago or more, there were other big cats similar to cheetahs in this genus, but today, the cheetah is one of a kind!

Question 6: What about house cats? What genus are they a part of?

Is it...

A: Lepardus

B: Felis

Do you have it? Ready for the answer?

The answer is... B!

Small cats are part of the *Felis* genus. Since members of the Felidae are called *Felid*, that means that your feline is a felis and a felid. Feline, felis, felid. Say that ten times fast!

The scientific name for cat is *felis catus*. "Felis" comes from the Latin word "felix" which means happy, just like "feliz" in Spanish means happy. So *felis catus* just means happy cat!

Question 7: During which historical era did the first cat appear?

The world has had many important times in history, including ice ages and the times of the dinosaurs. Where do ancient cats fit in?

Is it…

A: The Mesozoic

B: The Cenozoic Era

Do you have it? Ready for the answer?

The answer is… B! The Cenozoic Era.

Way back, over 25 million years ago, the first cats existed in the Paleogene Period, which was in the Cenozoic Era and long after the dinosaurs went extinct.

The first cat to be found in North America was called the Pseudaelurus, and this cat was around the same size as house cats today! This ancient cat is known as the ancestor cat for all of the living cats today.

Question 8: What do all cats, and many other animals, have in common?

Big and small cats are part of a bigger group of animals that all have certain traits in common. What is it?

Is it…

A: Cats are mammals

B: Cats are invertebrates

Do you have it? Ready for the answer?

The answer is... A! Cats are mammals.

All cats—big, small, gentle, scary—are all mammals. To be a mammal, an animal has to have a backbone, three middle ear bones, fur or hair, the ability for the moms to make milk, and a neocortex, which is a part of the brain.

Question 9: What do big and small cats have that help them sneak up on prey?

Cats are predators and hunters. To catch a meal, they need to be very quiet. What do they have that help them be stealthy as they hunt?

Is it...

A: Bushy tails that hide noise with their swish

B: Retractable claws

Do you have it? Ready for the answer?

The answer is... B!

Cats have retractable claws, which means that their claws are not always out and ready to scratch. This helps them keep their claws safe, so that they don't hurt their claws when they're not using them. And, it helps them silently go up to what they are trying to hunt. It's also part of why you may not hear a cat coming to see you, either!

So because house cats have a lot in common with the big wild ones, these small cats have some wild behaviors! Have you noticed any? Let's see what behaviors these cats have that helped them live in the wild!

Question 10: Why do cats hiss?

There is a specific reason why cats hiss! Cats are very good communicators, and they can mew, chirp, meow, and make all sorts of noises. So why do they hiss?

Is it…

A: They want to blend in with the sound of a rushing river

B: They are trying to sound like snakes

Do you have it? Ready for the answer?

The answer is… B!

Cats are pretending to be snakes! Cats are smart, and they can be little actors, playing a role. Cats know that many creatures are afraid of snakes, even though snakes are not the biggest animal in the wild. Small cats want to sound intimidating and threatening, so that they can be the one to scare whatever feels scary to them in the moment—whether that's a dog, another cat, a human, or anything that makes them think "now would be a really good time to hiss."

Question 11: How fast can cats run?

When we think of going fast, we think of a cheetah. Wow, are cheetahs fast! But cheetahs are a cat! A big cat. What about small cats? How fast can your cat go?

Is it…

A: 10 miles per hour

B: 30 miles per hour

Do you have it? Ready for the answer?

The answer is… B! 30 miles (or 48 kilometers).

Cats are so fast, that if we were in a car at the same speed of a cat, and we drove past a school zone, we would get pulled over and told no, we can't do that! I can't run 30 miles per hour, can you? That is faster than most professional cyclists, people who ride bicycles for sport!

No wonder your cat zips around the room when your cat has the zoomies!

Question 12: Cats walk in a specific way—first on either their right or left legs, then the other side. What other animals walk in this way?

Is it…

A: Zebras and chimpanzees

B: Giraffes and camels

Do you have it? Ready for the answer?

The answer is… B!

Even though giraffes and camels are not cats, cats have something in common with these animals that live in hot weather. Out of all of the animals in the whole world, only cats, giraffes, and camels walk with one whole side of their body moving together and then the other side of the body catching up.

Fun fact: a catwalk, that models do when walking on a runway, was named after the smooth way that cats walk—one side, and then the other.

Cats In The Wild Mini-Quiz

Here is your recap question for cats in the wild:

Lions, tigers, jaguars, leopards, snow leopards, and even cheetahs and cougars are called what type of animal?

Do you remember?

Big cats!

Now that we know some fun facts about the cat family and some of the neat history and behaviors they have in common, let's go even deeper into cats and their bodies. What makes cat bodies so special and different from humans? You're about to find out!

3
Cats And Their Bodies: Part 1

Cats can be big, small, or tiny like newborn kittens. But one thing is for sure: cats have different bodies than humans do, and they have some interesting facts about their bodies that are helpful for humans to know!

Because there are so many fun facts about cats and their bodies, this section is split into two chapters right here in Volume 1, and another two chapters in Volume 2. Get excited, because there is a lot to learn.

Let's play a game called TRUE or FALSE. When I read a question, you will shout out the answer: either "true" or "false." Got it? Ready? Let's play!

Question 1: Cats are fully colorblind

True or false? Cats are fully colorblind.

Did you say your answer?

The answer is… FALSE.

This is a tricky question! Cats do not see colors like humans do. But, they do not see only in black and white, either. Cats may be red-green colorblind and see colors like yellows, blues, and grays, so they do see some colors even if they don't see the full rainbow of colors that humans get to see. So they might not help you out with your Christmas decorations, but they can see your favorite yellow or blue T-shirt.

Question 2: Cats can hear better than some dogs

We know that dogs' hearing is much better than humans'. But what about cats? Is their hearing even better than dogs'?

What do you think? How good is a cat's hearing?

True or false? Cats can hear better than some dogs.

The answer is… TRUE!

For hearing, we measure sounds in hertz, and sometimes kilohertz. Humans, like you and me, can hear sounds up to 20 kilohertz. Not bad. It lets us listen to music, and learn really cool facts like these facts about cats!

Dogs can hear twice as well as humans! Dogs can hear sounds up to 40 kilohertz. That's why when someone talks in a really high pitched voice, you might hear a joke that they're making sounds only a dog could hear! There are even dog whistles that humans can't hear but make dogs come running!

But cats can hear sounds up to 60 kilohertz. That means that when someone is coming to your door, your cat will hear their footsteps well before you do! And even if you are talking in another room, your cat can probably hear you.

Question 3: Cats have fewer taste buds than humans do

Cats have strong senses, right? Their sense of smell is so good! What about taste?

True or false? Cats have fewer taste buds than humans do.

The answer is… TRUE!

Humans have 9,000 taste buds and cats have… wait for it… 473. 9,000 versus 473! That is a big difference. No wonder that you and your cat have different ideas about what foods taste good!

Question 4: Humans have a stronger sense of smell than cats do

You know when the cat's litter box is not smelling good, but it doesn't seem to bother the cat!

True or false? Humans have a stronger sense of smell than cats do.

The answer is… FALSE!

Humans have five million odor sensors in their noses. Can you guess how many cats have, if humans have five million? Five million is a lot, right? How many do you think cats have? Eight million? Ten million? Twenty million?

Cats have 200 million odor sensors. 200 versus 5! There is no question that cats can smell better than humans!

Question 5: Cats have a third eyelid

We humans have two eyelids. What about cats?

True or false? Cats have a third eyelid.

The answer is… TRUE!

Not only do cats have a third eyelid, but scientists believe that humans used to have a third eyelid, too, and that eyelid went away as humans evolved over time. The third eyelid on cats helps protect the cats' cornea, which is a part of the eye.

Question 6: Cats have 30 toes

Humans have… how many toes? What's the count?

Five over here, five over here. Ten toes. What about cats?

True or false? Cats have 30 toes.

The answer is… FALSE!

Cats do have more toes than humans do because they have four paws to walk on and humans have two feet and fingers instead of toes on our hands. But cats do not have 30 toes! Cats have 18 toes. Cats have five toes on their two front paws and four toes on their two back paws. Five plus five plus four plus four equals… did you get it? 18.

Question 7: Humans have more bones in their bodies than cats do

Humans are much bigger than many cats. Our fingers are bigger, our toes are bigger, and our brains are bigger. The brains of cats are the size of a human pinky finger, and their brains weigh less than a plum, the purple fruit. But do humans also have more bones?

True or false? Humans have more bones in their bodies than cats do.

The answer is… FALSE!

Humans have 206 bones, but cats have 230 bones in their little bodies! As many as 19 to 23 of these bones are in their tail alone!

Question 8: Cats have knees, elbows, and ankles

When we look at humans, our knees and elbows stick out a lot. What about cats? Do they have them too?

True or false? Cats have knees, elbows, and ankles.

The answer is… TRUE!

Just like humans, cats have two knees, two elbows, two ankles, two wrists, and even two kneecaps.

Cats' knees and elbows are much higher on their bodies than knees and elbows in humans, so many people get confused and think that their knees are the bent part above the cat's paw. But the bend above their paws are actually still part of their feet. The knees and elbows are closer to the core of the cat's body.

Cats have kneecaps, too, and the kneecaps are only on their rear legs. Their elbows on their front legs do not have this extra bone.

Question 9: Cats' collarbones are connected to their backbones

Maybe you've heard the song about the bones of the human body that are connected to each other. Since cats have so many bones, are they all connected, too? We know that their foot bone is connected to their leg bones. What about their collarbones?

True or false? Cats' collarbones are connected to their backbones.

The answer is… FALSE!

Collarbones in cats are found in the muscles of their shoulders. That means that the collarbones aren't connected to any other bones in their body! Their detached collarbones make it so that cats can squeeze into very small spaces—spaces as small as their heads!

Question 10: Cats' whiskers are more than just hair on their face

We see cats' whiskers on their faces. Do they have more whiskers on their body?

True or false? Cats' whiskers are more than just hair on their face.

The answer is… TRUE!

Cats have whiskers on their upper lip, above their eyes, on their chin, and on the backs of their front legs. The whiskers are as wide as the cat's body and are as sensitive as the fingertips of humans. Whiskers help cats make sense of the world around them, and also can communicate to humans when a cat is happy or afraid. It's important to never cut a cat's whiskers and to be gentle when playing.

Question 11: Cats have a higher body temperature than humans do

Some humans who have cuddly cats call them their personal hot water bottles. Cats are mammals, and mammals make their own internal heat. But are cats hotter than humans?

True or false? Cats have a higher body temperature than humans do.

The answer is… TRUE!

Humans average a temperature of 97 to 99 Fahrenheit (which is around 37 degrees Celsius). Cats have a body temperature between 100 and 102 degrees Fahrenheit (or around 38 degrees Celsius). That's why when you hold a cat on your lap, it may feel warmer than you are. It's also why cats want to be warm and snuggly, resting on blankets or on your lap. Any warmth outside helps the cat stay warm inside.

Question 12: Humans have a faster heartbeat than cats

Just because humans are bigger than cats, does that mean that their hearts beat faster?

True or false? Humans have a faster heartbeat than cats.

The answer is… FALSE!

Cats have the faster heartbeats. Not only do cats have a faster heartbeat than humans, but their heartbeat might be extra fast when going to the vet, because the kitty may be nervous. In general, their heart beats 140 to 220 beats per minute, which is over twice as fast as most human heartbeats.

Cats and their Bodies, Part 1 Mini-Quiz:

Here is your recap question for cats and their bodies, part 1:

What is the bone that cats have that is not connected to other bones in their bodies?

Do you remember?

The collarbones.

Ready to keep going? The next chapter has even more facts about cats and their bodies. Keep your trivia hat on. Let's go!

4
CATS AND THEIR BODIES: PART 2

Question 1: Cats age differently than humans do

Human years start with being a baby, then a toddler, then just a kid for a long time, and eventually, way, way down the line, an adult. What about cats? Is it the same?

True or false? Cats age differently than humans do.

The answer is… TRUE!

Cat years are not all the same, when we compare them to human years. When a kitten turns one years old, that cat is developmentally similar to a human that is 15 years old. That is a lot of things to learn in just one year!

After two years, the cat is developmentally equivalent to a 25-year-old human.

Then, for each year after that, every cat year is about four human years. So a four-year-old cat would be similar in human years to 33 years old.

That is a lot of math to say that cats age in a different way than humans do. Cats do a lot of learning and growing in the first two years of their life, and then they are adults!

Question 2: Cats have smaller eyes relative to the size of their heads than most animals

Some cats love to make eye contact, so you may have spent some time looking in those pretty cat eyes! But how big are they?

True or false? Cats have smaller eyes relative to the size of their heads than most animals.

The answer is… FALSE!

Compared to all other mammals, which are animals like humans, whales, and dogs, cats have the largest eyes when comparing the eyes to the size of their heads. The better to see you with! Let's take a look at that and see how well cats can really see.

Question 3: Cats see distances better than humans do

With the largest eye-to-head ratio of any mammal, surely cats see more clearly than humans do.

True or false? Cats see distances better than humans do.

The answer is… FALSE!

Cats see objects as blurry both when the objects are very far away and when the objects are very close. They are considered nearsighted and also farsighted. They can't see well very far away and wait to hunt until their prey is within a closer range. Up close, cats' vision is around 20/100, which in humans is considered low vision and on the way to legally blind. So if you put a toy or a treat right in front of their face, they might not see it very well.

But, cats do have stronger vision than humans in a couple of ways. First, the peripheral vision of cats, how they see from side to side, is much wider than that of humans. Cats have a peripheral vision that is 20% more than humans, so they can scan almost all the way around as they hunt in the wild. Second, their night vision is better than humans', and cats can hunt in the dark just like they can in the daytime.

Question 4: There's a reason why cat eyes are so shiny

Have you ever seen a cat caught under a light or flashlight in the dark and noticed how bright the cat's eyes were?

True or false? There's a reason why cat eyes are so shiny.

The answer is… TRUE!

Cats have another layer of tissue in their eyes, unlike humans. This extra layer is called *tapetum lucidum*, and it helps reflect the light into the cats' eyes to give them better night vision. This layer helps the cat, and also adds that special glint into their eyes that humans can admire!

Question 5: Humans can wiggle their ears better than cats can

Our ears are good for hearing and even for doing some tricks, sometimes! Maybe you have a friend who can wiggle their ears.

True or false? Humans can wiggle their ears better than cats can.

The answer is... FALSE!

Cats have fantastic control of their ears. Cats have a part of their ear called the *pinna*, which captures sounds and also can move in many directions. 32 muscles in the ear can rotate the pinnae 180 degrees. That is halfway around! And the pinnae on each ear can move separately, so the ears don't have to move at the same time. When the pinnae rotate, the cat can better hear sounds all around.

Question 6: Cat's paws are very sensitive

Cats jump onto rooftops, down from refrigerators, and use their paws to play with toys and prey. But are their feet actually sensitive?

True or false? Cat's feet are very sensitive.

The answer is... TRUE!

Even though cats don't wear shoes like humans do, paws don't have hair or calluses so that cats can sense what is going on in the world through their paws. The information that they get through their paws is so specific that they can even learn about prey who are hiding in the ground! But, all of this sensitivity in their paws means that they don't usually like humans to touch their paws.

Question 7: Cats have a fingerprint on their paws, like humans do on their fingers

Every human has fingerprints that no other human has. Is it the same for cats?

True or false? Cats have a fingerprint on their paws, like humans do on their fingers.

The answer is… FALSE!

Cats do have a unique fingerprint, that only that cat has and no other cat has. But it's not on its paws. Can you guess where it is? What is the most unique part of a cat? It's its nose! A cat's nose is unique to that cat only. When you see your cat's nose, you can know that no other cat in the whole world has a nose exactly like that!

Question 8: Male and female cats are righties

Do you write your name or play catch with your right hand or your left hand? Like humans, cats are righties or lefties, too! They may not be writing their own name on paper, but they will reach for a toy or to scratch with a certain paw.

True or false? Male and female cats are righties.

The answer is… FALSE!

Male cats and female cats have different paw preferences! Female cats, like many humans, tend to be righties, so they reach first with their right paw. Male cats, on the other hand–literally—tend to be lefties. Because of this, male cats might be more fearful. A study showed that cats who are lefties or who use both paws equally showed more fear than cats who were righties. So, beyond just what your cat likes to do, which paw your cat uses more may help explain why one cat is more afraid than another cat.

Question 9: Cats have two different types of hair

We know that cats have more than one type of hair, right? There is the fur and the whiskers.

True or false? Cats have two different types of hair.

The answer is… FALSE!

Cats have whiskers that are called vibrissae. The other types of hair are called down, guard, and awn hairs. Down hair is the soft, short undercoat. Guard hair is the longer outer layer. And awn hair is longer than down hair but shorter than guard hair and helps to protect the coat. With so many different types of hair, no wonder cats need to spend so much time grooming!

Question 10: Some cats don't respond to catnip

Cats can have a very strong and excited reaction to catnip. But does that happen to every cat?

True or false? Some cats don't respond to catnip.

The answer is… TRUE!

Up to 50% of cats—that's up to half of all cats!—do not react at all to catnip. It's genetic—some cats have the genes that make them love catnip and some don't. And kittens younger than 3-6 months old also do not respond to catnip, even if they will when they get a bit older.

But, there are other ways that your cat can have a similar experience to catnip even without these genes. Some other things to try are silver vine or a shrub called Tatarian honeysuckle. There was a recent study that found that one in three cats did not react to catnip, but that from the cats that did not have any reaction, 75% of them responded to silver vine. That is a huge percentage! And to Tatarian honeysuckle, one third of the cats who didn't react to catnip did have a reaction to this shrub. So there are many chances for your cat to have these fun experiences.

Question 11: Cats can have allergies to people

Some people are very allergic to cats. Some humans are allergic to certain flowers, or foods, too. Can cats have allergies in the same way?

True or false? Cats can have allergies to people.

The answer is… TRUE!

Cats can be allergic to many things, including things around humans. Some cats are allergic to human dandruff, which is not always easy for the human to control. Other cats are allergic to cigarette smoke or dust around the house, and some cats have asthma just like some humans do. Only one in 200 cats are estimated to have asthma, but if you or your cat have allergies in the home, getting some fresh air will help both of you!

Cats and their Bodies, part 2: Mini-Quiz

Here is your recap question for cats and their bodies, part 2:

What age is a cat that is about developmentally equal to a 15-year-old human?

Do you remember?

Just one year old. When a kitten turns one, it has developed as much for a cat as a 15 year old has for a human.

Now that we've talked about body traits and behaviors for all cats, let's go even deeper into specific cats and learn about different cat breeds and color patterns.

5
FACTS ABOUT CAT BREEDS AND COLORS

Do you have a cat? Do you know what kind of cat you have? Or do you just know a color—you have a black cat, or a gray cat, or even an orange cat!

Dog breeds are very different—think of all the differences in size and color from a poodle to a golden retriever. But what about cats? Cats have fascinating facts about their breeds, too!

Let's play a round of TRUE or FALSE. I will state a so-called fact, and you will shout out the answer—if you think the answer is right or wrong. True or false.

Question 1: A Maine Coon is the largest house cat

If you've ever seen a Maine Coon, you'll know that they are fluffy cats! Their fur makes them look even bigger than they are! But are they the biggest?

True or false? A Maine Coon is the largest house cat.

The answer is… TRUE!

Some people say that MAYBE a savannah cat is bigger, but they're not sure if a savannah cat is really a domesticated cat, so as far as house cats go, the Maine Coon is the biggest! A Maine Coon cat was in the Guinness Book of World Records for being almost four feet long from head to tail. That is a big cat!

Question 2: Some Maine Coons have six toes

A cat that has more toes is called a polydactyl cat. Is that true of a Maine Coon?

True or false? Some Maine Coons have six toes.

The answer is... TRUE!

Because Maine Coons are so large, and they used to be outside in the snow, many of their ancestors had six toes—some think that 40% of them, almost half of early Maine Coons, had six toes! This helped them balance and grip better with their paws. Today, most Maine Coons have the regular number of toes, but some do have six.

Question 3: Bombay cats were originally from India

Bombay used to be the name for a city in India now called Mumbai. Are these black cats from India?

True or false? Bombay cats are Indian.

The answer is... FALSE!

Today's Bombay cats were bred in the United States, breeding sable Burmese with black American Shorthairs.

Bombay cats are always black, and no other breed has this color and sheen. The person who created the breed of Bombay cats, Nikki Horner also called them "Patent-Leather Kids with the New-Penny Eyes" because their black coats and copper-colored eyes were so shiny. Some people give them another nickname: a small black panther, because they look like small wild cats.

In fact, that's why they were given the name Bombay—because that's an area where black panthers, which Bombay cats were bred to look like, can be found.

Question 4: The smallest breed of cat is called the Munchkin

Like the people in the Wizard of Oz, or the very small donut holes, this cat breed may be smaller than others! But is it the smallest?

True or false? The Munchkin is the smallest breed of cat.

The answer is… FALSE!

It turns out Munchkin cats are only a little smaller than other cats. The smallest cat breed in the world comes from Asia in the country of Singapore. The breed is called Singapura, and compared to an average house cat, the Singapura is half of the size!

If you want a teeny tiny cat, a Singapura cat weighs about 5 pounds or less, loves to cuddle, and is an expert climber and athlete!

Question 5: There are 100 different cat breeds

Dogs have 340 pedigreed breeds. What about cats? If cats are the most popular pet, and cats are on every continent on earth except for Antarctica, how many breeds of cats are there?

True or false? There are 100 different breeds of cats.

The answer is... FALSE!

Even though there are hundreds of different dog breeds, there are only 42 pedigreed cat breeds. Now, pedigreed means that it doesn't include every possible combination of cat, only the ones that officials have called purebred. So if your cat is a stray and looks a little different from these 42, your cat may be one of a kind. But for other cats, cats are likely only one of 42 different kinds of cat. Do you know all of them? I'll list the 42 and you can shout "YES" when you have heard of this breed of cat!

1. Abyssinian
2. American Bobtail
3. American Curl
4. American Shorthair
5. American Wirehair
6. Balinese
7. Bengal
8. Birman
9. Bombay
10. British Shorthair
11. Burmese
12. Burmilla
13. Chartreux

14. Colorpoint Shorthair
15. Cornish Rex

How many have you said "yes" to? Can you count? Here are some more.

16. Devon Rex
17. Egyptian Mau
18. European Burmese
19. Exotic
20. Havana Brown
21. Japanese Bobtail
22. Korat
23. LaPerm
24. Maine Coon
25. Manx
26. Norwegian Forest
27. Ocicat
28. Oriental
29. Persian
30. Ragamuffin

How about these ones? Have you heard of any of these cat breeds? Here's our last few.

31. Ragdoll
32. Russian Blue
33. Scottish Fold
34. Selkirk Rex
35. Siamese
36. Siberian

37. Singapura

38. Somali

39. Sphynx

40. Tonkinese

41. Turkish Angora

42. Turkish Van

42 breeds of cat is not hundreds like dogs have, but that is still a lot of cats!

Let's talk about colors! Did you know that the color of a cat does not always mean that it is part of a different breed? Just like a Labrador can be black, brown, or yellow, and there are lots of black dogs of different breeds, cats too can have different colors either in the same breed or across different breeds.

Question 6: A "tabby" cat is a pattern, not a breed

We hear about tabby cats more than we hear about many breeds of cats. But is a tabby not even a breed of cat?

True or false? A tabby is a pattern, not a breed.

The answer is… TRUE!

Tabby is a cat that has a particular gene called an agouti gene. Fun fact: an agouti is another animal that lives in Central and South America! But in this case, the agouti is the name of the gene that these cats have. If a cat has the agouti gene, the cat can have four types of coats, meaning coloring patterns on its fur.

The most common pattern of a tabby is called a mackerel, and the other types are the classic tabby, the ticked tabby cat, and the spotted tabby cat.

Most tabby cats have an "M" shape of their stripes in the middle of their forehead, and most tabby cats are striped and look like little tigers! But the ticked tabby cat does not have a striped pattern on its coat.

Tabby cats can be American Shorthairs, British Shorthairs, Maine Coons, and many other breeds of cats!

Question 7: Most orange tabby cats are female

Fun fact: all orange cats are tabby cats! Every one! So your little orange tiger or lion is a tabby! Another fun fact is that orange cats are sometimes called velcro cats because they love to snuggle.

So what is it? True or false? Most orange cats are female.

The answer is… FALSE!

4 out of 5 orange cats, which is 80%!, are male. Now, that leaves 20% of orange cats that are female, so there are plenty of female orange cats looking for cuddles. But if you see an orange cat, chances are, it's a male cat.

The reason for this is in the chromosomes. Females need two X chromosomes where the parent cats pass on their orange genes, but males have XY chromosomes and only need the mom cat to pass on the orange genes.

Question 8: Calico and tortie cats are male

Just like a tabby cat, a calico is not a breed of cat but rather a type of coloring and patterning in its fur.

Calico cats have a tri-colored fur pattern, usually white, black and orange. Tortie cats, or tortoiseshell cats, have two colors that aren't white.

True or false? Calicos and tortie cats are male.

The answer is… FALSE!

Calico and tortie cats are 99.9% female. Why? Because having those beautiful colors—two different colors from white, that both calico cats and tortie cats have—need two X chromosomes. So why are calico cats female? It's in their genes! The kind that tells you what you look like, what color eyes you have, and what color hair you have.

For calico cats, almost all of these colorful cats are female cats.

Cat Breeds and Colors Mini-Quiz

Here is your recap question for cat breeds and colors:

What is the name of the largest breed of house cat?

Do you remember?

The Maine Coon.

High five! You know so much about cats, different kinds of cats, and even wild cats. But what about your cat? Do you know what your cat is telling you and if your cat is a happy cat? Find out the signs your cat gives you!

6
HOW TO TELL IF YOUR CAT IS HAPPY

You want your cat to be happy, right? Chances are, with a loving human friend like you, your cat is a happy and very lucky cat! There are some ways that you can be more sure, though. Everyone likes a happy, silly, goofy cat!

Let's play a game called THIS or THAT.

For each question, I will give you TWO options, and you have to choose your answer. You say THIS if you choose the first one, THAT if you choose the second, or BOTH if you think both options are true.

Let's get started!

Question 1: Why does your cat rub against you?

Have you ever stood in the kitchen and had your cat walk directly at you, just to rub against you and then walk away? What does this mean? Why does your cat rub against you?

THIS: to mark its territory

THAT: because your cat is happy!

What do you think? THIS, THAT, or BOTH?

The answer is… BOTH!

When your cat is happy and loves being around you, your cat will rub up against you. Its little body will rub up against your feet and legs, and when you're sitting down, your cat might rub its cheek against you. Your cat is happy, and saying hi! Your cat is also leaving behind some oil on you, so that other cats know that you are taken! You belong to your cat!

Question 2: What does your cat do with its mouth and throat when it is happy?

Your cat makes sounds and eats with its little head and throat. What can you look for to know if it's happy?

THIS: Your cat purrs!

THAT: Your cat bites you!

What do you think? THIS, THAT, or BOTH?

The answer is… THIS!

When your cat purrs, it is a sign that your cat is a happy cat and is happy to be around you!

Question 3: Which way does your cat point its tail when your cat is happy?

Your cat's tail may be always moving or swishing around. What can it tell you about your cat? Where is the tail when your cat is happy?

THIS: Your cat points the tail down to the floor

THAT: Your cat's tail is straight up and a little wiggly

What do you think? THIS, THAT, or BOTH?

The answer is… THAT!

When your cat walks up to you, tail straight up to the sky, a little shaky like it is full of so much energy, that means that your cat is so happy to see you!

Question 4: What does your cat do with its paws to show you it's happy?

Your cat has four paws and it likes to use them! It likes to use its paws with you, too! What can its paws tell you about how happy your cat is?

THIS: it claws you gently, in a way that could also be called "kneading" or "making biscuits"

THAT: it swats its claws at you!

What do you think? THIS, THAT, or BOTH?

The answer is… THIS!

Making biscuits, or kneading you, is a sign that your cat is happy and having fun. Just be careful that the claws don't go too deep. Your cat sometimes doesn't know the power of its own claws!

Question 5: What sound does your cat make when it's happy?

Meow, hiss, chirp, growl. Your cat makes a lot of sounds! For some of them, like hissing, you can just tell that your cat is not so happy. But what sounds does your cat make when it's happy?

THIS: your cat meows at you in a high pitch when you walk through the door

THAT: your cat chirps in a way that sounds like a mix between a chirp and a meow

What do you think? THIS, THAT, or BOTH?

The answer is… BOTH!

Cats have over 100 vocalizations, meaning the sounds that they make. That is a big vocabulary for a little animal! Some of these sounds let you, their human friend, know that they are happy and happy to see you. If you hear these little chirps and get greeted by a quick meow, your cat is telling you it is happy you are here!

Question 6: What can the litter box tell you about your cat?

You know when you need to change the litter box! Taking care of the litter box is one of the main ways you look after your cat. But could it tell you something about your cat's mood?

THIS: your cat is happy

THAT: your cat is sick or stressed

What do you think? THIS, THAT, or BOTH?

The answer is… BOTH!

How your cat uses the litter box can tell you a lot about your cat! If your cat is not using the litter box but leaving you presents somewhere else, something is going on! But if your cat is using the litter box regularly and everything is going well, then you can feel happy knowing that your cat is a happy cat!

Question 7: how does your cat look at you when it's happy?

Your cat may love to look at you. After all, cats are curious and want to know what is going on! How do you know what the stare means? What is a happy stare?

THIS: your cat stares at you without blinking

THAT: your cat looks at you and blinks slowly

What do you think? THIS, THAT, or BOTH?

The answer is… THAT!

For humans, we blink a lot! We need to blink when our eyes are dry. For cats, blinking is a sign of vulnerability, because they are not watching for danger when their eyes are closed! If your cat blinks at you, you know that your cat trusts you and is feeling safe and happy.

Question 8: How does a happy cat eat?

Did you know that when a cat doesn't like the food, the cat just won't eat it! Now that is a strong will! But what about when your cat is eating? What does that tell you? Is it happy?

THIS: Just a little bit—your cat wants to stay small to fit through mouse holes!

THAT: Excitedly at every meal—your cat loves food!

What do you think? THIS, THAT, or BOTH?

The answer is… THAT!

When your cat doesn't eat well, your cat may be stressed, sick, or just not like the food. But when your cat can't get enough of that kibble or wet food, your cat is happily finding that life tastes good!

Question 9: If your cat's coat is shiny and well-groomed, what does that mean?

Your cat spends more than half of its day grooming! If the fur is gleaming, and your cat is quite busy keeping it styled just so, what does that tell you about your cat?

THIS: your cat is bored of grooming and wants your attention

THAT: your cat is happy and is taking good care of itself

What do you think? THIS, THAT, or BOTH?

The answer is… THAT!

If your cat has its fur sticking straight up, dirty, not taking care of itself, you might want to look closer because your cat may be sick, stressed, or sad. But if your cat's coat is glossy and glorious like a cat supermodel, then you have one happy cat!

Question 10: What shape does your cat's tail look like when it's excited?

Your cat's tail can make a lot of funny shapes! Just like you can move your arm in all directions, so can your cat use its tail to tell you a thing or two about what is going on! So what is a sign that your cat is happy? What shape does it make with its tail?

THIS: a question mark

THAT: a triangle

What do you think? THIS, THAT, or BOTH?

The answer is… THIS

When your cat is happy and confident and thriving, your cat may hold its tail straight up and then bent at the tip to one side. This looks like a question mark, but there is no question here. This is a happy cat!

Question 11: What does your cat want to do when it's happy?

Your cat has a lot of needs! It sleeps, eats, grooms, hunts for crawly things in the house. But when your cat is happy and relaxed, what does your cat want to do with you?

THIS: cuddle with you

THAT: play!

What do you think? THIS, THAT, or BOTH?

The answer is… BOTH

Signs that your cat is happy include cuddling with you and playing–with or without you! When your cat snuggles with you in bed, or is sitting on your lap, your cat is loving your affection and just being with you! How lucky your cat is to be with you!

When your cat is darting around the room, playing with toys, or swatting at the string you are holding, your cat is happy to be at ease and living its best life.

Happy Cat Mini-Quiz

Here is your recap question for how to tell if your cat is happy:

What does it mean when a cat can't wait to eat the cat food that you put in the bowl?

Do you remember?

It means the cat is happy!

Cats have attitude—or cattitude—but there are things that we humans can feed them or not feed them to keep them happy. Keep reading to find out what foods cats can't get enough of and what foods they should stay away from.

7
FOODS CATS LIKE AND HATE

Cats love to sleep, groom themselves, play, and eat. What do they like to eat? What do they not like to eat? Let's play a game of TRUE or FALSE to understand what foods could make a cat purr and what foods could make a cat hiss.

Question 1: Cats are vegetarians

People can be meat eaters, vegetarians, vegans, or some sort of combination or in between. For humans, we know that eating our veggies is good and healthy for us! What about cats?

Do cats love chomping on lettuce and carrots, like bunnies? True or false? Cats are vegetarians.

The answer is... FALSE!

Cats are called "obligate carnivores" which means that they need meat to survive. Cats can't be vegan just like cows can't be meat eaters—it's not good for them! Cats need a high-protein diet and the specific compounds that meat has. And, cats have a hard time digesting carbohydrates, which are high in foods like bread, pasta, and fruits and vegetables. Cats can have a couple vegetables, and we will see that, but it's meat that makes cats happy, healthy and thriving.

Question 2: Cats love cantaloupe

We just said that cats love meat, but what about this orange melon? Cantaloupe is great on its own or, for us humans, mixed in a fruit salad. But what about cats?

True or false? Cats love cantaloupe.

The answer is… TRUE!

Even though to us, cantaloupe tastes sweet and like a fruit, to cats, they notice something else going on with cantaloupe! Cantaloupe has some of the same amino acids, which are the molecules that are in protein, as meat does! This means that when cats are sniffing with their excellent sense of smell, to them, cantaloupe smells meaty!

Question 3: Eating raw salmon is good for cats

As humans, sometimes we eat raw fish and call it fancy words like sashimi, or lox, or carpaccio. Cats like fish, right? What about raw fish?

True or false? Eating raw salmon is good for cats

The answer is… FALSE!

Cooked salmon is very healthy for your cat, and it is in many packaged cat food options. You can even give some cooked salmon to your cat off of your plate! But when it comes to raw salmon, it's not good for your cat. First, eating raw salmon is risky for your cat and may give it food poisoning. But even if there isn't bad stuff in there, raw fish has an enzyme that breaks up a B vitamin called thiamine, and cats need that vitamin. Without it, they could be very sick.

So for cats, cooked salmon is fantastic, and raw salmon can be cooked before giving it to your cat!

Question 4: Cats can become addicted to tuna

Opening up a can of tuna fish is a surefire way to get your cat to come running! But is there such a thing as too much of a good thing?

True or false? Cats can become addicted to tuna.

The answer is… TRUE!

Cats love tuna, but too much of anything is not always best. Tuna has a strong flavor that cats love and may decide to choose that over anything else. Tuna alone does not give cats all of the nutrition and vitamins that they need to be strong and healthy cats, so they do need to eat other things besides just tuna. Keep giving other foods to your cat to remind them that there are more foods than just tuna fish!

Question 5: Cats hate spinach

Cats are carnivores and spinach is a vegetable! The cartoon Popeye loves spinach, but what about cats?

True or false? Cats hate spinach.

The answer is… FALSE!

Many cat foods have spinach in them! Your cat may or may not like chomping on spinach, but the vitamins in spinach are good for cats. Some of the vitamins that cats need and love are A, C and K, iron and calcium, and those are all in spinach. In cat food, spinach is often mixed in with meat to make the leafy green a little more tasty for these meat eaters!

Question 6: Cats can eat some human breakfast food

Eggs, oatmeal, bananas. That's what humans like to eat. What about cats? Do they want to come to the diner with us?

True or false? Cats can eat some human breakfast food.

The answer is… TRUE!

Cats can eat eggs, bananas, and oatmeal! The eggs are a good source of protein and B vitamins but the eggs should always be cooked. The bananas are a healthy treat, but should only be given in very small amounts to cats, because cats should eat their meat first before having a snack like bananas. And oatmeal, like spinach, is already in many packaged cat foods! Not every cat likes all of these foods by themselves, so it's important to just give your cat a little taste whenever trying anything new so that your cat can tell you, "yum, I like it!" Or "blech, not for me, thanks."

Question 7: Pumpkin can be a health food for cats

True or false? Pumpkin can be a health food for cats.

The answer is… TRUE!

Since pumpkin is high in fiber, some vets suggest pumpkin when a cat is having tummy troubles. The vitamins and fatty acids in pumpkin are also good to keep the cat's fur healthy, and the vitamin A, potassium and iron help with its overall health. Many cat foods that are in stores have meals that include pumpkin in them so that your cat gets a little extra help when it needs it.

Question 8: Fatty meats are best for cats

Do cats do best with lots of fat on their meat and skin on the bones, or with lean cuts that don't have any of that?

True or false? Fatty meats are best for cats.

The answer is… FALSE!

Cats do best with lean meats without skin or fatty areas. Some human foods that cats like include chicken and turkey, because they are lean and have the protein that cats like. Just make sure that the meats don't have too much salt on them and don't have any other spices.

Question 9: Garlic, onions, chocolate, grapes, and raisins are bad for cats

True or false? Garlic, onions, chocolate, grapes, and raisins are bad for cats.

The answer is… TRUE!

The best food for cats is food that is specifically labeled cat food. These foods have all of the right nutrients and vitamins and none of the other stuff. But if your cat ever pokes around at human food, here are the foods to avoid:

Garlic and onions. Humans love these flavors. Cats need to avoid them! Whether in vegetable form or from a spice shaker, cats cannot eat garlic and onions.

Chocolate is often a favorite food of some humans, in a bar, in candy, in hot chocolate, or even in ice cream! But for cats, chocolate is a no-no. If you are sipping hot cocoa and a cat walks by you, make sure to keep your cup far from the curious cat!

Grapes and raisins. These fruits and dried fruits are another food to avoid for cats.

Question 10: Cayenne pepper is deadly to cats

Chocolate, garlic, grapes are all very bad for cats. But what about the spicy red pepper that we put on food sometimes?

True or false? Cayenne pepper is deadly to cats.

The answer is… FALSE!

Technically, cayenne pepper is not as bad for cats as the other foods. However, eating cayenne pepper will make cats very sick, and having the pepper on their paws or furs will cause them irritation and even pain. Cats know this, so when they smell cayenne pepper, they run away! Sometimes if people don't want wild cats in their backyard, these humans will put cayenne pepper on the ground. Cats smell the pepper and decide to stop going to that house. So even though cayenne pepper isn't totally deadly, it's not good for cats!

Question 11: Cats and dogs can share food

How many different types of food and bowls do you need in one house, if you have a cat and a dog?

True or false? Cats and dogs can share food.

The answer is… FALSE!

Cats and dogs need different types of nutrients and can't get everything they need from eating each other's food. For example, cats need meat to survive, but dogs can live on a vegetarian diet. Dogs can eat more carbohydrates like fruits and vegetables and bread than cats can. The main things that cat food has that dog food does not are meals high in taurine, protein, vitamin A, and a compound called arachidonic acid. Since dogs don't need these as much, their food just doesn't focus on that. Cats and dogs can each have their own separate food and meals even if they live in the same house.

Foods Cats Like And Hate Mini-Quiz

Here is your recap question for foods cats like and hate:

What foods should cats never have? See if you can name three.

Do you remember?

Chocolate, garlic, onions, grapes, and raisins.

Cats are special critters with big personalities. Some specific cats have wowed and fascinated humans. Ready to learn about some famous cats? Keep reading to see which cats became celebrities, in the next chapter.

8
CATS WHO BECAME FAMOUS

If you have a fur baby, you may know that your cat thinks they are the most important cat in the world. And they are! Every cat is a big deal! But some cats have made history because someone, or many people, said, that is one cool cat. Let's find out who they are!

Now, this section is more advanced than the other chapters. If you are ready for a challenge and to learn some more history, see if you can follow a thing or two about real cats today and from many years ago.

For this game, I will ask one question and read two answers, and you will choose the correct answer!

Are you ready to learn about some famous cats? Let's go!

Some cats stole our hearts in movies! Let's go through some very notable cats that we saw on TV.

Question 1: In the Harry Potter movies, how many cats played Mrs. Norris, Mr. Filch's cat?

Is it..

A: 4

B: 10

What do you think?

The answer is… A!

Four different Maine Coons took turns acting in the Harry Potter movies, because they had different skills. One was really good at standing still, another was trained to walk and then stop at different spots, another could easily jump on the shoulders of Mr. Filch, and the last one was trained to look all around when directed. Three of the four cats were rescue cats, and now they are all living their best cat lives as movie stars.

Question 2: In the animated Disney movie The Aristocats, what is the name of the song the musician cats sang?

Is it…

A: "I'm a Cat and I Don't Care"

B: "Ev'rybody Wants To Be A Cat"

What do you think?

The answer is… B!

The Aristocats is a movie from 1970 that has a lot of cats in it, including the rich cats that are the main characters. But for the other people and animals, the song "Ev'rybody Wants To Be A Cat" was a hit. In this movie, the cats helped each other out, and some of the humans helped out the cats, too!

Let's go back to historical times. Who are the cats who have made history?

Question 3: Ancient Egyptians loved cats so much that they did what with cats?

Is it…

A: Held big, fancy weddings where they had a boy cat marry a girl cat

B: Worshiped a half-feline goddess

What do you think?

The answer is… B!

Not only did ancient Egyptians have a goddess named Bastet, who was feline, but a whole city was made just to celebrate this goddess! Ancient Egypt also buried cats in tombs and gave them offerings just like they would important humans, except for the cats, they gave offerings like mice and milk! And if anyone harmed a cat, that person was terribly punished. Ancient Egypt knew how to respect cats!

Question 4: Author Ernest Hemingway loved cats. What was the name of his most famous cat?

Is it…

A: Fuzzy

B: Snowball

What do you think?

The answer is… B!

A ship captain gave Snowball to Hemingway and one of the things that made Snowball special was that Snowball had extra toes—Snowball was a polydactyl cat! Hemingway decided to get more, and started collecting polydactyl cats, these cats with extra toes! In fact, Hemingway's love for polydactyl cats was so famous, that these cats are sometimes called Hemingway cats. Today, at the Hemingway Museum in Florida, there are around 50 cats wandering around and being taken care of at the museum, and that includes many polydactyl cats!

Question 5: Why was a cat named Tom called a war hero?

Is it...

A: Tom the cat found food supplies when everyone was hungry

B: Tom hissed at the enemy and won the war

What do you think?

The answer is... A!

In the Crimean War way back in 1855, no one could find food in the town of Sevastopol and everyone was very hungry. But Tom the cat was healthy with a gleaming fur coat. Where was Tom getting food? Tom led the troops to a pile of rocks, and underneath the rocks was a big supply of food, enough to feed everyone! Tom was celebrated as a hero and a soldier adopted him as a pet.

Question 6: What famous inventor created the first known cat video?

Cute cat videos are all over the internet, and maybe there are some that you watch over and over! But did you know that cat videos have a place in history?

Is it...

A: Benjamin Franklin

B: Thomas Edison

What do you think?

The answer is... B!

Thomas Edison invented the light bulb! This very important and ingenious inventor also had another, lesser-known invention: he invented viral cute cat videos. In 1894, he videotaped a "boxing" match of two cats in a ring. How cute!

How about in recent times? Are there famous cats today? There sure are!

Question 7: Tardar Sauce is a cat that went viral starting in the year 2012 for her face that always seemed to be in a mood. What is the name that the internet gave to Tardar Sauce?

Is it...

A: Sad tabby

B: Grumpy Cat

What do you think?

The answer is… B!

Grumpy Cat was a sensation in memes all over the internet, but her owner swears that Grumpy Cat is a very happy cat, and she just looks grumpy because that's just how her face looks!

Question 8: What breed of cat has the Guinness World Record for the longest cat?

Is it…

A: Ragamuffin

B: Maine Coon

What do you think?

The answer is… B!

The longest cat is a Maine Coon named Barivel, at 3 feet and eleven inches! (1.2 meters)

Question 9: What age has the Guinness World Record as the oldest cat?

Is it…

A: 25 years old

B: 38 years old

What do you think?

The answer is… B!

Crème Puff lived a wonderful life of 38 years with his owner!

Cats are clearly very loved. And many of them have also done very important things in the world!

Question 10: Has a cat ever been to space?

Is it…

A: Yes, a rocket launched a cat to space

B: No, cats stay here on earth!

What do you think?

The answer is… A!

Back in the 1960s, space travel was very important to a lot of people. They sent a dog named Laika to space, then a chimpanzee named Ham, and then a cat from France! This cat's name was Félicette, although she was sometimes called Astrocat because of her 15 minutes trip when she spent 100 miles above this planet (160 kilometers). Now, Félicette is celebrated in a 5-foot (1.5 meters) bronze statue at the International Space University in a town in France called Strasbourg.

Question 11: In what US state did a cat serve as mayor of a town for 20 years?

A cat as a mayor of a town? That sounds silly, right? But it's true! Which state do you think this happened in?

Is it…

A: Tennessee

B: Alaska

What do you think?

The answer is… B!

A town named Talkeetna in Alaska had a mayor named Mayor Stubbs. Stubbs was an orange tabby who didn't have a tail. He ran for office and no one ran against him, so he stayed mayor for 20 years, with high approval ratings!

Question 12: In what country does a cat manage a train station?

Is it…

A: Mexico

B: Japan

What do you think?

The answer is… B!

In Japan, a cat named Nitama is called a "stationmaster." Before Nitama, another cat named Tama managed the station, so since "ni" means "two" or "second," Nitama is the second Tama and now is a fun sight to see when people come from all over the world to meet the cat stationmaster. Nitama's job is to make the train passengers happy during their commute—the cat leaves the paperwork for a human to handle.

Famous Cats Mini-Quiz

Here is your recap question for cats who became famous:

What did Thomas Edison invent, besides the light bulb?

Do you remember?

Cute cat videos.

It's time to move on to the lightning rounds, two super-speedy quizzes to see how many cat facts you remember. Let's do it!

9
FINAL TRIVIA QUIZ: EASY LIGHTNING ROUND

Are you ready for a lightning-fast, super quiz to test you on what you know about cats? Random order. Let's get started!

Question 1: What kind of animal are cats? Mammals or reptiles?

Mammals! Cats are mammals

Question 2: Are cats vegetarians or meat eaters?

Cats are meat eaters, or carnivores. Cats need to eat meat.

Question 3: Are there more pet dogs or pet cats in the United States?

Pet cats. There are millions more pet cats in the United States.

Question 4: What is the largest house cat?

The Maine Coon is the largest house cat.

Question 5: What can't cats taste? Sour, sweet, or bitter?

Sweet. Cats cannot taste sweetness.

Question 6: What is your cat telling you when it bends its tail into the shape of a question mark?

That it's happy. When a cat's tail is shaped like a question mark, it is happy.

Question 7: Should cats eat raw fish, like salmon?

No, cats should stick to cooked fish and cat foods.

Question 8: What is the name of the hit cat song from the movie The Aristocats?

"Ev'rybody Wants To Be A Cat." The name of the song from The Aristocats is "Ev'rybody Wants To Be A Cat."

Question 9: What kind of fruit do cats enjoy because it tastes like meat to them?

Cantaloupe. Cantaloupe smells similar to meat to cats.

Question 10: What part of a cat's body is as unique to cats as a fingerprint is to a human?

The nose. The nose of a cat is as unique as a fingerprint is to a human.

Question 11: Can cats enjoy chocolate?

No, chocolate is very bad for cats. Cats should not eat even a little bit of chocolate.

Question 12: What is a clowder?

A clowder is a group of cats.

Question 13: What is the name of the smallest breed of cat?

The Singapura. The Singapura is the cat breed.

Question 14: What type of fish can be addictive for cats, because it tastes so good to them?

Tuna. Cats can become almost addicted to tuna fish and not want to eat other food.

Question 15: What is the gender of orange tabby cats?

Male. Orange tabby cats are male cats.

Question 16: What breed of cat played Mrs. Norris in the Harry Potter movies?

Maine Coon. Mrs. Norris in the Harry Potter movies was a Maine Coon.

Question 17: What type of meat is best for cats: lean meat or fatty meat?

Lean meat is best for cats.

Question 18: What is the name for a group of kittens?

A kindle. A group of kittens is called a kindle.

Question 19: How do cats walk that is different from other four-legged animals?

Cats walk with both legs from one side of their body and then both legs of the other side of their body

Question 20: What other animals walk one full side at a time?

Giraffes and camels. Giraffes and camels also walk with both legs on one side of the body before using the legs on the other side of the body.

Question 21: This starchy, orange food can be good for cats and their digestion. What is it?

Pumpkin. Having pumpkin in their diet can be healthy for cats and their digestion.

Question 22: Cats have this condition that makes them not digest milk well. What is it?

Lactose intolerance. Cats are lactose intolerant and cannot digest milk well after they wean, just like some humans.

Question 23: What kind of claws do cats have that help them sneak up on prey?

Retractable claws. Cats have retractable claws.

Question 24: What country used to love cats so much that worshippers had gods that looked like cats?

Egypt. Ancient Egypt had gods that took on the shape of cats.

Question 25: What are some animals that are big cats? Name three. I'll wait a second while you list them.

Lions, tigers, jaguars, leopards, snow leopards, and even cheetahs and cougars are all names of big cats.

Question 26: What kinds of cats are the names of color patterning, not pedigreed breeds of cats?

Tabby, calico, and tortoiseshell are names of patterning, not breeds. The color of a cat is not the same as the breed of a cat.

Question 27: What red, green, or purple fruit should cats never eat?

Grapes. Cats should never eat grapes, or their dried version, raisins.

Question 28: What is the name for a male cat?

A tom. A male cat is called a tom.

Question 29: What is the name for a neutered male cat?

A gib. A neutered male cat is called a gib.

Question 30: What is the name for a female cat?

A molly. A female cat is called a molly.

Question 31: What human breakfast foods can cats eat? Can you name one or two?

Eggs, bananas, and oatmeal. Cats can eat eggs, bananas, and oatmeal and may or may not like those foods.

Question 32: What part of a cat's body has tons of nerve endings and is more sensitive than a cat's fur?

Whiskers. Whiskers are more sensitive than a cat's fur.

Question 33: Should cats eat dog food?

No, cats should not eat dog food, because cats need different nutrients than dogs do.

Question 34: What do big cats in the Panthera genus do that house cats do not?

Roar. Big cats like lions and tigers roar, while house cats purr.

Question 35: What traits do cats have that make them mammals? Name three. I'll give you a few seconds.

To be a mammal, an animal has to have a backbone, three middle ear bones, fur or hair, the ability for the moms to make milk, and a neocortex. A cat has all of these.

Question 36: What is the name that people on the internet called a cat named Tardar Sauce who had an interesting expression?

Grumpy Cat. Grumpy cat's real name is Tardar Sauce.

Question 37: If humans have two eyelids, how many do cats have?

Three. Cats have three eyelids.

Question 38: What viral cat trend did Thomas Edison invent?

Cute cat videos. Thomas Edison started the trend of cute cat videos.

Question 39: What animal are cats imitating when they hiss?

A snake. Ancient cats knew to imitate the sound of a snake, and cats today instinctively know how to do that.

Question 40: What is the name of Ernest Hemingway's famous cat?

Snowball. The cat that he loved so much was named Snowball.

Question 41: Do cats only see in black and white and not in color?

Cats see some colors. Cats may be red-green colorblind so they see yellows, blues, and grays.

Question 42: Which cat is probably a leftie, male cats or female cats?

Male cats.

Question 43: What bones are detached from other bones and are found in the muscles of their shoulders, so that cats can squeeze into tight spaces?

Collarbones. Collarbones are found in a cat's shoulder muscles and aren't connected to other bones.

Question 44: In a town in Japan, a cat is a stationmaster. What is the type of station that the cat manages?

A train station. In a town in Japan, a cat manages a train station.

Question 45: What household spice do people sometimes put in their backyards to make cats go away because cats don't like it?

Cayenne pepper. Cats do not like cayenne pepper.

Question 46: What breed has the longest cats?

Maine Coon. The longest cat is a Maine Coon.

Last question of this round, question 47: How old is a one-year-old cat in human years?

A one-year-old cat is the equivalent of 15 human years old.

How did you do? Did you ace it, or miss a few? You can always go back and read it again to see the answers another time!

If you're ready, it's time to move on to the final and hardest quiz yet! Ready, set, go!

10
FINAL TRIVIA QUIZ: HARD LIGHTNING ROUND

Was the last round too easy for you? Do you want more of a challenge? This lightning round is hard! If you don't get it all the first time, you can read it again and test yourself. Here are extra advanced questions. Ready? Set? Go!

Question 1: What is the scientific name for cats?

Felis catus. The name for a domesticated cat is felis catus

Question 2: What percentage of genes do house cats share with a tiger?

95.6%. Almost 96% of the genes of a house cat are the same as the genes of a tiger.

Question 3: What is the name of the protein in dander that people who are allergic to cats are allergic to?

Fel d 1. The protein is called Fel d 1 and it's found inside of dander.

Question 4: What is the name of the cat family that includes all small cats and big cats?

Felidae. All cats are part of the felidae family.

Question 5: How many miles per hour can domesticated cats run?

30 miles per hour. Cats can run 30 miles per hour.

Question 6: What is the name of the Celtic festival in which a black cat would curse a house that didn't leave out some milk, that led to people thinking that black cats were bad luck?

Samhain. The festival called Samhain evolved into what we know of as Halloween today in the United States.

Question 7: What is the name of the genus that house cats belong to?

Felis. The name of the genus that house cats belong to is the Felis.

Question 8: Besides a clowder, what are two other names for a group of cats?

A clutter and a glaring are two other names for a group of cats. Clutter and glaring.

Question 9: What is the name of the extra layer of tissue on the cat's eyes?

Tapetum lucidum. The layer that makes cats' eyes shiny when hit with light is called tapetum lucidum.

Question 10: What is the name for the type of carnivores that cats are?

Obligate carnivores. Cats are obligate carnivores.

Question 11: How many toes does a cat have?

18 toes. Cats have 18 toes.

Question 12: What is a dowt and a destruction?

A dowt and a destruction are names for a group of wild, feral cats.

Question 13: Besides their upper lip, where else do cats have whiskers?

Above their eyes, on their chin, and on the backs of their front legs.

Question 14: Which big cat is the only cat in the genus Acinonyx?

Cheetahs. Cheetahs are the only cat in the genus Acinonyx.

Question 15: During which historical era did cats first appear?

The Cenozoic Era. Cats first appeared in the Cenozoic Era.

Question 16: Follow up, even harder question: during which epoch in the Cenozoic Era did cats first appear?

The Paleogene Period. Cats first appeared in the Paleogene Period in the Cenozoic Era.

Question 17: What was the name of the first cat to be found in North America, that all living cats descended from?

Pseudaelurus. The Pseudaelurus is the ancestor of all living cats today.

Question 18: Félicette was a famous French cat. What was she famous for?

Félicette went to space. Félicette was the first cat to go to space.

Question 19: What is a cat's vision measurement when seeing objects up close?

20/100. Cats have a vision of 20/100 up close.

Question 20: In what country does a cat at your door mean luck and that you may receive money?

Scotland.

Question 21: How many bones does a cat have in its body?

230 bones. Cats have 230 bones in their body.

Question 22: Tom the cat was a war hero. What did he do that gave him the praise of being a war hero?

He found a food supply that helped make sure that everyone had enough to eat.

Question 23: How many ear muscles does a cat have?

32. A cat has 32 ear muscles.

Question 24: What is a normal body temperature for cats, in either Fahrenheit or Celsius?

100 and 102 degrees Fahrenheit or around 38 degrees Celsius.

Question 25: Ernest Hemingway loved a certain type of cat with six toes that is sometimes called Hemingway cats. What is the name?

Polydactyl cats. Hemingway loved polydactyl cats, which have six toes.

Question 26: How old was the oldest cat, Crème Puff?

38 years old. Crème Puff the cat was 38 years old.

Question 27: In a town in Alaska, a cat served as mayor for 20 years. What was the name of this cat?

Mayor Stubbs. Mayor Stubbs was listed as mayor in a town for 20 years.

Last question, question 28: What percentage of a cat's body is water?

60-70% of a cat's body is water.

You made it! How many answers did you get? If you missed some answers—or many answers—don't worry! You can always read it again until you get every answer right! You have learned so much just by reading.

A QUICK NOTE

Have you learned a thing or two about cats? If you learned some facts about cats by reading this book, purr-ty please leave a review!

Just scan the QR code below and write a few words about what you learned about cats.

That's it!

Your words are so lovely for a new author like me and help me write more fun books that humans can read to learn about the fascinating world of cats!

Thank you for your help, and for your love of cats!

CONCLUSION

You are a cat expert, now! Do you know how many facts were in this book that you just read? Do you think it was more than 20 or less than 20? More than 100? 120? Well, you have learned over 170 facts about cats—small cats, big cats, and even movie star cats.

Did you follow along through the lightning rounds? How many times did you read it? Reading facts more than once is a great way for some of those facts to set in so that you remember them long after you finish this book. But even if you read it just one time, some of those facts will stick with you!

What was your favorite thing you learned about cats? Did any facts stand out to you as extra interesting?

Did you like learning about the cat's body and the science and biology? Did you like learning about why cats do the things they do, like show you they're happy or eat certain foods? Was it interesting to hear about the famous cats, like the internet star or the heroes or the cat who was the mayor of an entire town?

You may have heard some things that you have in common with cats. Maybe you like pumpkin and spinach and tuna fish like cats do, and you love playing with your cat.

And you may have heard some things that are very different from you and cats. For example, you may love chocolate and your cat can't eat chocolate. Or you love to be in close spaces, like cuddled up under the blankets, but your cat can fit into much smaller spaces because of the way the bones in its body are. And you walk differently. Can you imagine if you crawled on all fours and moved your whole body with your right hand and foot first and then your left hand and foot only after that? It takes some good balance to walk like a cat!

Cats are smart and very loving when they want to be—just like you! The fun fact that you completed a trivia book means that you are a smart and curious learner, and that curiosity and interest in learning will take you very far, wherever you go and whatever you decide to learn next!

There are so many fun facts about cats that I couldn't include them all in one book—believe me, I tried!—so this is Volume 1. Volume 2 has even more facts, even more cats, and more advanced knowledge.

Before you go, please remember to write a review on Amazon so that more cool cats can find this book and learn some purr-fectly fascinating facts about cats!

If you want to be the first to know about new kids trivia books and audiobooks, you can send a quick email to ashmalarkeybooks@gmail.com.

Thank you for reading and for learning more about our four-legged friends!

REFERENCES

6 Small Cat Breeds That Will Always Stay Kitten-like | Purina. (n.d.). Retrieved 29 October 2022, from https: //www.purina.co.uk/find-a-pet/articles/cat-types/breed-guides/small-cat-breeds

8 of the Biggest Domestic Cat Breeds | Purina. (n.d.-a). Retrieved 29 October 2022, from https: //www.purina.co.uk/find-a-pet/articles/cat-types/breed-guides/big-cat-breeds

10 Cat Breeds That Are the Most Affectionate. (2022, September 21). The Spruce Pets. https: //www.thesprucepets.com/affectionate-cat-breeds-4846595

10 of the Most Famous Cats Throughout History | Purina. (n.d.). Retrieved 29 October 2022, from https: //www.purina.co.uk/articles/cats/behaviour/common-questions/famous-cats-in-history

50 Cat Facts You Probably Didn't Know. (2021, November 4). Georgia Veterinary Associates. https: //www.mygavet.com/services/blog/50-cat-facts-you-probably-didnt-know

101 Amazing Cat Facts: Fun Trivia About Your Feline Friend in Charlottesville, VA. (2018, July 5). Charlottesville Cat Care Clinic. https: //cvillecatcare.com/veterinary-topics/101-amazing-cat-facts-fun-trivia-about-your-feline-friend/

Alden, J. (2022, July 5). *What Is A Group Of Cats Called? | Learn more on Litter-Robot Blog.* https: //www.litter-robot.com/blog/what-is-a-group-of-cats-called/

All About Cats Editorial. (2022, June 19). *Toybob: Small Cats With Big Loving Hearts.* All About Cats. https: //allaboutcats.com/toybob

All About Hemingway Cats: The Cats With Extra Toes. (2022, July 8). Michelson Found Animals Foundation. https: //www.foundanimals.org/all-about-hemingway-cats-the-cats-with-extra-toes/

Are Cats Right- or Left-Pawed? How To Tell. (2022, January 24). https: //www.litter-robot.com/blog/are-cats-right-or-left-pawed/

Betty Currie News - The New York Times. (n.d.). Retrieved 29 October 2022, from https: //web.archive.org/web/20081219194150/http: //topics.nytimes.com/top/reference/timestopics/people/c/betty_currie/index.html?inline=nyt-per

Blue Cross. (n.d.). 12 common cat myths debunked. Retrieved 29 October 2022, from https: //www.bluecross.org.uk/advice/cat/12-common-cat-myths-debunked

Dol, S., Caspers, J., & Buckingham, L. (n.d.). Responsiveness of cats (Felidae) to silver vine (Actinidia polygama), Tatarian honeysuckle (Lonicera tatarica), valerian (Valeriana officinalis) and catnip (Nepeta cataria). National Library of Medicine. Retrieved 29 October 2022, from https: //pubmed.ncbi.nlm.nih.gov/28302120/

Bombay Cat Breed Information. (2015, July 24). Pet Blog - Dogs, Cats, Fishes and Small Pets Blog. https: //www.petsworld.in/blog/bombay-cat-information.html

Breeds – The Cat Fanciers' Association, Inc. (n.d.). Retrieved 29 October 2022, from https: //cfa.org/breeds/

Calico Cat: Breed Profile, Characteristics & Care. (2022, June 20). The Spruce Pets. https: //www.thesprucepets.com/calico-cats-profile-554694

Can Cats Eat Cayenne Pepper? Is It Safe or Toxic. (2020, December 9). Adventurous Cat. https: //adventurouscat.com/can-cats-eat-cayenne-pepper/

Cat Senses | PAWS Chicago. (n.d.). Retrieved 29 October 2022, from https: //www.pawschicago.org/news-resources/all-about-cats/kitty-basics/cat-senses

Cat Trivia: 41 Cat Facts for National Trivia Day. (2022, July 12). Michelson Found Animals Foundation. https: //www.foundanimals.org/cat-trivia-41-cat-facts-national-trivia-day/

Cellania, & Alan, A. T. (2014, April 13). Crimean Tom and Other War Cats. Neatorama. https: //www.neatorama.com/pet/2014/04/13/Crimean-Tom-and-Other-War-Cats/

Chewy Editorial. (2022a, February 28). Why Do Cats Lick You? Cat Licking Behavior Explained. BeChewy. https: //be.chewy.com/behavior-pet-body-language-why-does-my-cat-lick-me/

Chewy Editorial. (2022b, September 22). *15 Human Foods That Are Safe for Cats*. BeChewy. https: //be.chewy.com/nutrition-food-treats-15-human-foods-that-are-safe-for-cats/

Colgate. (2022a, September 20). *Foods that are Dangerous or Toxic to Cats.* Hill's Pet Nutrition. https: //www.hillspet.com/cat-care/nutrition-feeding/toxic-foods-for-cats

Crnec, J. M. A. I. (2022, April 15). 🐱 *DO Cats Have KNEES? What About ELBOWS And ANKLES?* MyCatTips. https: //mycattips.com/do-cats-have-knees-elbows-ankles-as-humans/

Cross, L. (2022, October 10). *Little-Known Facts About Top 10 Cat Breeds.* Vetstreet. https: //www.vetstreet.com/our-pet-experts/little-known-facts-about-top-10-cat-breeds

DiNuzzo, E. (2022, October 26). *Why Do Cats Love Boxes?* Reader's Digest. https: //www.rd.com/article/why-cats-love-boxes/

Do Cats Feel Love? | Comfort Zone. (n.d.). The #1 Brand in Cat and Dog Behavior Management. Retrieved 29 October 2022, from https: //www.comfortzone.com/behavior-blog/cat-behavior/do-cats-feel-love

Do Cats Have Nine Lives? The Origin of the Saying. (2022, January 24). https: //www.litter-robot.com/blog/do-cats-have-nine-lives/

Doctors, E. (2022, March 16). *6 Best Cat Breeds for Emotional Support.* ESA Doctors. https: //esadoctors.com/6-best-cat-breeds-for-emotional-support/

Drake, N. (2013, October 16). *This Is How Cats See the World.* WIRED. https: //www.wired.com/2013/10/cats-eye-view/

El, S. (2022, May 16). *How Many Pets Are In The World & The US? 71+ Pet Stats.* Simply Insurance™. https: //www.simplyinsurance.com/pet-statistics/

Fawcett, K. (2020, October 29). *Facts About Cats*. Mental Floss. https: //www.mentalfloss.com/article/578211/cat-facts

Fawcett, K. (2022, May 17). *12 Facts About Maine Coons*. Mental Floss. https: //www.mentalfloss.com/article/76734/12-huge-facts-about-maine-coons

Felis catus. (n.d.). Retrieved 29 October 2022, from http: //bioweb.uwlax.edu/bio203/s2009/aschenbr_rach/Classification.ht m

Fun Cat Facts for Kids. (2018, November 12). Traverse Mountain Pet Care. https: //traversemountainpetcare.com/fun-facts-and-information/fun-cat-facts-for-kids/

Fun Facts On Cats For Kids & Adults. (2020, August 4). Active Wild. https: //www.activewild.com/fun-facts-on-cats/

Gardner, L. (2022a, June 27). *Fun Cat Facts: 39 Fascinating Facts About Cats | Litter-Robot*. https: //www.litter-robot.com/blog/30-fascinating-cat-facts/

Gardner, L. (2022b, July 5). *Cat Allergies: Why Are So Many People Allergic? | Litter-Robot*. https: //www.litter-robot.com/blog/cat-allergies-why-are-so-many-people-allergic/

Gardner, L. (2022c, September 6). *Tabby Cats: Facts, Details, and Breed Guide | Litter-Robot*. https: //www.litter-robot.com/blog/tabby-cat-folklore-facts/

Gardner, L. (2022d, September 21). *Cat Years To Human Years: How Old Is My Cat? | Litter-Robot*. https: //www.litter-robot.com/blog/how-to-convert-your-cats-age-to-human-years/

Ghose, T. (2013, October 16). *Feline Vision: How Cats See the World.* livescience.com. https: //www.livescience.com/40459-what-do-cats-see.html

Gould, W. R. (2021a, July 28). *12 Telltale Signs Your Cat Is Happy.* Reader's Digest. https: //www.rd.com/list/happy-cat-signs/

Gould, W. R. (2022a, July 27). *50 Cat Facts That Are Purr-fectly Fascinating.* Reader's Digest. https: //www.rd.com/list/cat-facts/

Gould, W. R. (2022b, September 30). *Decode Your Cat's Behavior: 17 Cat Behaviors Explained.* Reader's Digest. https: //www.rd.com/list/how-to-decode-your-cats-behavior/

Gould, W. R. (2022c, October 12). *10 Noises Your Cat Makes—and What They All Mean.* Reader's Digest. https: //www.rd.com/list/cat-noises/

Handwerk, B. (2021, May 4). *House Cat Origin Traced to Middle Eastern Wildcat Ancestor.* Animals. https: //www.nationalgeographic.com/animals/article/house-cat-origin-traced-to-middle-eastern-wildcat-ancestor

https: //www.thedrakecenter.com/. (n.d.). *20 Amazing Facts About Cats.* The Drake Center for Veterinary Care. Retrieved 29 October 2022, from https: //www.thedrakecenter.com/services/cats/blog/20-amazing-facts-about-cats

Hutton, R. (2018, September 18). *The Surprising Story of the Only Cat Ever to Win the Highest Honor for Animal Military Gallantry.* Time. https: //time.com/5396568/simon-cat-war-medal/

Insurance, A. P. (2020, October 22). *Bombay Cat Facts.* https: //www.aspcapetinsurance.com/resources/bombay-cat

International Cat Care. (2020, November 23). *The Origins Of Cats*. https: //icatcare.org/advice/the-origins-of-cats/

Kelley, J. (2017, June 14). *5 Cool Cat Tail Facts*. Catster. https: //www.catster.com/lifestyle/cat-tail-5-cool-facts

Krouse, L. (2021, November 3). *Your Cat's Brain: 11 Crazy Facts You Didn't Know*. Great Pet Care. https: //www.greatpetcare.com/cat-behavior/your-cats-brain-11-crazy-facts-you-didnt-know/

Kuras, A. (2021, December 18). *101 cat facts: Fun trivia about felines*. Care.com Resources. https: //www.care.com/c/101-amazing-cat-facts-fun-trivia-about-your-feline-friend/

LeBeau, D. (2021, August 17). *The Orange Tabby Cat — 8 Fun Facts*. Catster. https: //www.catster.com/cats-101/orange-tabby-cat-facts

Maine Coon Central. (2022, April 8). *Is A Maine Coon Part Raccoon?* https: //www.mainecooncentral.com/is-a-maine-coon-part-raccoon/

Mann, S. B. (2021, August 19). *101 Great Cat Trivia Questions & Answers (+Facts)*. IcebreakerIdeas. https: //icebreakerideas.com/cat-trivia/

McCarthy, E. (2016, March 3). *11 Ways Big Cats Are Just Like Domestic Cats*. Mental Floss. https: //www.mentalfloss.com/article/57746/11-ways-big-cats-are-just-domestic-cats

myth. (2023, January 11). The Merriam-Webster.com Dictionary. https: //www.merriam-webster.com/dictionary/myth

NSTATE, LLC, www.n-state.com. (n.d.-a). *New Hampshire State Wildcat, Bobcat (Lynx rufus), from NETSTATE.COM*. Retrieved 29 October 2022, from https: //www.netstate.com/states/symb/wildcats/nh_bobcat.htm

NSTATE, LLC, www.n-state.com. (n.d.-b). *Official State Cats from NETSTATE.COM*. Retrieved 29 October 2022, from https: //www.netstate.com/states/tables/state_mammals_cats.htm

Osmanski, S. (2022, October 20). *The 21 Most Popular Cat Breeds in the U.S. If You're Looking for a New Feline Family Member*. Parade Pets. https: //paradepets.com/cats/most-popular-cat-breeds

Pets. (2022, October 24). Treehugger. https: //www.treehugger.com/pets-4846034

Polydactyl Cats: Origins, Care Tips & Fun Facts | Purina. (n.d.). Retrieved 29 October 2022, from https: //www.purina.co.uk/articles/cats/behaviour/common-questions/polydactyl-cats

So you're thinking about getting. . .a Ragdoll Cat. (n.d.). My Pet and I. Retrieved 29 October 2022, from https: //uk.mypetandi.com/new-owners/so-you-re-thinking-about-getting-ragdoll-cat/

Sorocco, E. (2021, June 18). *Toybob*. Catster. https: //www.catster.com/cat-breeds/toybob

species information. (n.d.). Retrieved 29 October 2022, from http: //www.catsg.org/cheetah/01_information/1_2_species-information/species-information.htm

Sung, M. W. S., PhD. (2022, August 25). *Why Do Some Cats Not React to Catnip?* PetMD. https: //www.petmd.com/news/view/why-do-some-cats-not-react-catnip-37525

The Cats Meow Caterwauling in Cats | VCA Animal Hospital. (n.d.). Vca. Retrieved 29 October 2022, from https: //vcahospitals.com/know-your-pet/the-cats-meow-caterwauling-in-cats

The facts behind cats' nine lives. (n.d.). Petplan. Retrieved 29 October 2022, from https: //www.petplan.co.uk/pet-information/blog/the-facts-behind-a-cats-nine-lives/

The History of the Domestic Cat. (n.d.). Alley Cat Allies. Retrieved 29 October 2022, from https: //www.alleycat.org/resources/the-natural-history-of-the-cat/

Top Breeds 2021 – The Cat Fanciers' Association, Inc. (n.d.). Retrieved 29 October 2022, from https: //cfa.org/cfa-news-releases/top-breeds-2021/

Toyger Cat: Cat Breed Profile, Characteristics & Care. (2022, June 30). The Spruce Pets. https: //www.thesprucepets.com/toyger-cat-profile-554213

Wahl, M. (2022a, July 27). *Can Cats See in the Dark?* Reader's Digest. https: //www.rd.com/article/can-cats-see-in-the-dark/

Walpole, D., & Nannestad, C. (2022, June 17). *Why Do Cats Lick You? Experts Offer 6 Possible Reasons.* Reader's Digest. https: //www.rd.com/article/why-do-cats-lick-you/

Why Can't My Cat Be Vegan? (2018, May 2). ASPCA. https: //www.aspca.org/news/why-cant-my-cat-be-vegan

Why Do Cats Have Whiskers? | VCA Animal Hospital. (n.d.). Vca. Retrieved 29 October 2022, from https: //vcahospitals.com/know-your-pet/why-do-cats-have-whiskers

Wikipedia contributors. (2022a, October 8). *PATSY Award.* Wikipedia. https: //en.wikipedia.org/wiki/PATSY_Award

Wikipedia contributors. (2022b, October 25). *Mammal.* Wikipedia. https: //en.wikipedia.org/wiki/Mammal

Wilson, J. (2022, March 22). *Cat Trivia, Facts and Information*. Cat-World. https: //cat-world.com/cat-facts-cat-information/

Wu, K. J. (2020, January 28). *Félicette, the First Cat in Space, Finally Gets a Memorial*. Smithsonian Magazine. https: //www.smithsonianmag.com/smart-news/felicette-first-cat-space-finally-gets-memorial-180974062/

PREVIEW OF TRIVIA FOR KIDS WHO LOVE CATS, VOLUME 2

This is just a small bit from a silly chapter from Trivia For Kids Who Love Cats, Volume 2, called "Why Cats Lick You."

You know when a dog sees you and gets so excited, and jumps up on you and even licks you?

Dogs are pretty clear about what they want and what they like. If they like you, they'll come close to you. If they are angry, they may snarl or growl or show their teeth.

But cats are a little more mysterious. Sometimes the way they act doesn't quite make sense to their human friends. So, we have a little code cracking to do.

Now, before we get into the game, here is a fun fact about cats. When dogs lick you, it might tickle a bit. But when a cat licks you, it is rough! It might not feel nice at all!

This is because cats have backward-facing hooks or spines called *papillae* that help them get more nutrients from the food they eat, including getting more meat off the bones. The hooks also help get debris off of their shiny coats, which is why they are always licking themselves.

So, if cats lick bones to scrape off more meat, and they lick their fur to get nice and clean, what are these felines doing licking humans?

Let's do a multiple choice test!

Multiple choice is a type of question we see a lot in tests in school and in quizzes online, like the quizzes on websites or apps. We see one question, and a few answers, and we have to choose which one is the right one. We only have one guess and then we know if we picked correctly! In this game, I'll read the question and answers and then repeat the question with the answers told in a shorter way so that you can quickly pick the letter next to the answer: a, b, c, or d.

Question 1: If your cat has a cat brother or sister and they lick each other, and your cat starts licking you too, what does that mean?

a) Your cat is hungry, and you look pretty tasty!

b) Your cat got lost on the way to the bowl

c) Your cat is bored and wanted to try something new

d) Your cat loves you and sees you as part of its inner circle of family

Well, what do you think? Why does your cat lick you like your cat licks other cats? Here's another way to look at these answers.

a) Your cat is hungry

b) Your cat is lost

c) Your cat is bored

d) Your cat has welcomed you into the inner circle

The answer is… D!

You are part of the cat family, just like the other cats that your cat loves so much.

Just as your cat will lick, head-butt, and nuzzle other cats, your cat will do the same to the cat's friends—human or not! You can feel honored that the cat sees you as part of its inner circle.

Question 2: If you're feeling sad, or you have a stuffy nose or a tummy ache and your cat is licking you more than usual, why is that?

a) Your cat is a positive cat only. No tears or sniffles here!

b) Your cat loves the taste of tears and boogers!

c) Your cat is a healer and wants you to have extra love and affection when you're feeling a little down.

d) Your cat is a curious cat, and any changes in your behavior makes the cat want to investigate, like a detective.

What do you think? Why does your cat lick you when you're sad or sick? Here's another way to look at these answers.

Is your cat:

a) Not letting you feel bad things

b) Hungry for tears and snot

c) Trying to cheer you up with love and affection

d) Curious and playing detective

Do you have your answer?

The answer is… C!

Your cat is a healer! Your cat senses that you are sad, or sick, or not feeling your absolute best, and your cat wants to help! Your cat knows when you aren't feeling well and will snuggle up next to you and, yes, even lick you!

And, it works! When you have your cuddly friend by your side, you start to relax and feel better! What a smart cat.

Question 3: Why does your cat lick you when your cat is feeling nervous?

a) Licking you helps them feel less stressed
b) Licking you means they are angry with you
c) Licking you is a sign that a mouse is nearby
d) Licking you means that the nervousness is because they don't like their food

Did you get it? What is it? Why does your cat lick you when feeling nervous? Here's another way to look at these answers.

a) You help them feel better
b) They're mad at you
c) They're ready to chase a mouse
d) They want better food

The answer is …

A!

Licking you helps them feel less stressed. Cats lick themselves to groom, but also when they are feeling stressed. Because cats are bonded to you, their owner, they may also lick you because it helps them feel connected and more secure. It's something that your cat can do to feel a little calmer and safer. So if you are getting some extra licks from your cat, you can know that your cat is feeling more at ease because you are around!

You now know some things about a cat's tongue and certain cat behavior. But what about the rest of the cat's body? What about other mysterious behaviors? Let's learn more...

THANK YOU FOR READING!

Here are some quick links for more cat and trivia fun:

Get your cat coloring book.

Share a review on Amazon (thank you!).

Share this book with someone you care about.

About the Author

Ash is a kid at heart with a big dream of bringing as much fun and fun learning to kids and kids at heart as possible. When Ash was 11, Ash wrote a 60-page book, fully illustrated, about grammar. Ash studied Creative Writing at the University of Pennsylvania and went on to work with artists and Fortune 500 companies before returning to the first love: words. Ash is the proud parent of a sassy Boston Terrier, godparent to two rescue cats, and also speaks French, Spanish, and German.

Made in United States
Troutdale, OR
10/10/2023

13582966R00072